DRAWN FOR FRIENDS

Drawn for Friends

Sketches and Verses
by
Joan Wanklyn·

 Threshold Books

© Joan Wanklyn 1986

First published in Great Britain 1986 by
Threshold Books Limited
661 Fulham Road
London SW6 5PZ

British Library Cataloguing in Publication Data
Wanklyn, Joan
   Drawn for friends.
   1. Horses—Pictorial works
   I. Title
   599.72'5   QL737.U62
ISBN 0-901366-53-6

Typeset by Falcon Graphic Art Limited
Wallington, Surrey
Printed in Great Britain by
Mackays of Chatham Limited

Contents

Introduction

This is unashamedly a lighthearted hotchpotch of sketches, many of which originated as my Christmas cards over the last thirty-odd years. Some appeared in their original form complete with verse – sorry, 'verse' sounds too pretentious, 'jingle' would be more appropriate! In other cases, the rhyming wouldn't jell until after the last date of posting before the appropriate Christmas. So this is the first occasion on which text and drawings have been fully married up.

Without the kindness of friends and relatives in lending back original drawings so that the printers could reproduce them afresh, there wouldn't have been a book. Nor could it have happened without the initial suggestion and continuing encouragement of my publisher, Barbara Cooper, and the help of all at Threshold Books.

Thank you *all*. It's been a 'fun project', and if it helps readers – or perhaps I should say friends old and new – to pass a few minutes pleasurably, it will have been worthwhile.

JW

FOR JO
who shared the fun

Wise Man from Afar

Not rich with alchemy of stars
Nor treasure chests nor bullion bars,
Not clad in damask or brocade
Nor bearing gifts of pearl or jade,
An ageless man with kindly hands
Beside a waiting pony stands.
Old eyes that watch the world unfold,
In him his forebears' skills re-told . . .
One, wise in way of man and beast,
Syce to the Magi from the East?

Teams

Coach and carriage and limber,
    Wagon and wain and dray,
Teams for hauling timber,
    Teams to plough all day,
Strong shoulders straining,
    Traces stretching taut –
Loyal and uncomplaining,
    The game and gallant sort.

See the proud manes tossing
    Or coats all streaked with sweat,
Soaked from a river crossing
    Or desert dry – and yet
How the steel links jingle
    How lamplit brasses gleam,
How strong and gentle mingle
    In the team, in the team.

The Pony who Taught us to Fall

I'll give you a toast!
It's to those who could boast
(If they chose) of deeds splendid or small:
Say, a season's fast polo
Or Badminton solo
Or clearing that famous red wall.

Let's drink to the winners,
The big money-spinners –
And remember all those who 'just missed'.
If they ran a good race
Even though short of pace
Then we'll honour them all on the list.

For, bumper or barger
Or troop horse or charger
Or pony who taught us to fall,
There's only one test –
Did they give of their best?
And if so, raise your glass – Bless 'em all!

Lad's Eye View

'There's some rum 'uns in our yard,
　　Nags you'd cross off any card –
Though the guv'nor lands a Seller where he can.
　　We've a hurdler off his corn
　　And a chaser all forlorn
That's tipped his jockey off each time he ran.
　　We've a colt who's Derby bred
　　But he'll likely lose his head
And wreck the flamin' stalls before the off.
　　We've shiverers and weavers
　　And flattering deceivers –
And I'm sure I heard that filly give a cough . . .
　　But this little 'un I do –
　　He's a winner through and through
And it won't be long before he's in the frame.
　　You could say I'm just a mug
　　But I've got the racing bug –
Hope springs eternal in this flippin' game!'

Coster Year

With his Uncle Jim's old trolley
And his little bay mare Dollie
He'd tramp around the houses big and small,
In the winter yelling 'Logs!'
Fit to waken all the dogs –
There never was a boy with such a bawl.

In the spring 'Old rags and iron!' –
Any junk was worth a try on –
Till sunny May would call a change of tune.
'Here's petunias and gloxes
For yer tubs and window boxes!'
Then strawberries in punnets most of June.

In September 'Best manure –
Keeps yer roses sweet and pure!'
Come October it was back to logs again.
But December – ah December,
That's the best month to remember –
With a sprig of mistletoe in Dollie's mane.

See the shabby little trolley
All festooned about with holly
And Christmas trees all smelling freshly green,
And the folk would seem more friendly,
And Dollie, munching gently
Was the greediest coster pony ever seen!

Glimpse

I glimpsed him, where he used to sit
    Below the drystone wall
To smoke a pipe and dream a bit
    Where willow herb grew tall.

A sack to keep his shoulders dry
    A bottle of cold tea
And memories of times gone by –
    Two dogs for company.

The dusty team beyond him stand
    Coats whorled with drying sweat:
Barley and Brock and Melisand,
    Chestnut and grey and jet.

I glance again – there is no wall
    No willow herb, no team –
Only an arid motorway
    NOT the right place to dream!

Magic Time

O, once upon a magic time
    Before the world grew old,
When sailor suits and button boots
    Were worn – or so I'm told –
When cooks were fat, and coachmen sat
    Behind two bang-up bays,
And talk flew fast as port was passed,
    Recalling hunting days.
When lamps were lit and men would sit
    To polish hame and link
And horses ploughed and then would crowd
    Into the pond to drink . . .
O, that was an enchanted time
    With all the stage to fill.
While childhood dreamed, it almost seemed
    That time itself stood still.

Salutations

It could be the lift of a courteous hat
In the hansom days of yore;
A persuasive 'Prrr?' from a thirsty cat
As the milkman comes to the door;
A ribald exchange on the broad highway
'Twixt postboy and toff on the box,
Or a cheerful wave for the lame and grey
From a tubful of chips from old blocks.
Whatever the motive or manner or means –
Cheek, charm or genuine cheer –
A greeting adds warmth to a wealth of scenes,
Most of all at the turn of the year.

Quest for the Elusive

'And now,' said the Chairman of the Big Company, peering at his notes, 'we come to the question of our next prestige calendar. Last year it was the Theatre, this year Horses. I have here a suggestion from our PR people that next year it should be British Mammals. Any comments?'

'Mammals,' nodded the Board, bored.

And mammals it was.

So the PR Manager whistled up an aspiring artist, who was told to go round the country at the Company's expense and come back with twelve paintings to include as many animals as possible, from imposing ones like grey seal and red deer, down to hedgehogs and stoats and weasels.

Off the artist went, to visit zoos and nature reserves and

26

private collections of animals, starting off with five days of scrambling up and down the great glens of Affric and Cannich, being briefed by a Forestry Commission ghillie on likely haunts of wild cat and pine marten, admiring the enlightened badger gates provided by the Commission to give those animals free passage from one enclosure to another, and making sympathetic noises when shown the damage roe deer can do to young trees.

It was October, and the hoarse gothic challenges of red stag carried for miles through the majestic valleys, above the background music of running water, from burn or torrent, cascade and river – and it rained almost incessantly.

Nonetheless the sketchbooks began to fill with studies of glens and rivers and moors, of pine trees and rocks and ferns – but not of animals, except the distant red deer. Even what had seemed a marvellous stroke of luck misfired. News had come that a disorientated young otter had wandered into the factor's office of one of the big estates, from whence it was rapidly removed to an empty stable. But only hours before it was due to be sketched the otter recovered from whatever had ailed it and escaped.

And then in a chance conversation somebody mentioned that a garage proprietor in Morayshire had a collection of animals. The telephone in the Fishers' Hotel was red hot before the garage was located, but located it was and hot foot – or rather hot tyred – the artist set off, getting a puncture en route and limping into the garage as a genuine customer as well as a seeker after knowledge.

The 'collection' in fact consisted of two animals, but both were beautiful and manna from heaven for a frustrated penciller. One was an adult roe buck, who had his own frustrations. He was sleek and fat and physically in splendid fettle, able to graze and exercise to the length of the light chain attached to his leather collar. But although the roe rut in summer, from the look in his hot brown eyes there was still but one thought in his mind – does. And clearly the next best thing would be to impale one of those irritating humans on the dagger spikes of his short but lethal antlers. So the artist sat on an old tool box just out of reach and drew and drew, while the buck picked daintily at tempting morsels of food in between

churning up the damp earth first with one antler, then with the other.

And then there was Donal, the wild kitten. Half grown, probably of feral not truly wild stock, but beautifully marked and with the flattened ears and withdrawn expression so characteristic of wild cats – and which can even be glimpsed in domestic felines when they lose patience with their human slaves.

Poor Donal. Life was bleak for her (from her face she was almost certainly female). They weren't deliberately unkind to her, but until it was decided what to do with her she was kept in a very small wire netting run – the kind of run a hen and chicks, or a somnolent Belgian hare or a family of guinea pigs might be happy in, but a cat – never. They shut off her haylined sleeping box so that she could be sketched by the artist, who found her cold stare uncomfortable, and tried to make amends by bringing her the next morning, in a paper bag, a share of the fried liver produced by the small hotel for 'tea'.

It worked – or nearly. With a lightning movement Donal seized the small piece of liver that dropped through the top of the wire netting, sniffed it and devoured it with despatch, and then – shortlived triumph – looked straight up at the artist in an obvious enquiry. Eagerly the artist dropped more liver through the wire, and again Donal's lightning paw shot out. But this time disaster. Her dewclaw caught in the wire netting floor of the cage and the more she tugged to free it the more firmly the wire became hooked in the claw, stretching it painfully away from the forearm. The artist watched, eyes stung by hot, helpless tears, and cursing the stupid impulse to drop the liver through the wire. At last, after what seemed an age, the claw was freed and the kitten retreated to the far corner of the tiny cage, shaking the hurt paw at intervals, ignoring the liver and directing a stare of cold mistrust towards her unwitting tormentor, who, demoralised, quickly completed the sketches and prepared to leave.

But what to do about Donal? What could be done? Purchase her and her cage, load it on to the roof rack of the little car, and take it up to the wildest bit of moorland and release her – but to what sort of fate? The garage proprietor was in Inverness, and there was so little time if an appointment was to be kept with the curator of Edinburgh Zoo next morning. So many excuses for doing nothing . . . and the artist drove away trying to forget but not succeeding.

There were two genuine wild cats at Edinburgh Zoo in a big enclosure with rocks and branches. And an otter cub who played in and out of her pool and seemed to take pleasure in having an attentive audience of one, as well as in the gleaming, freshly caught fish of her evening meal. The artist, being inquisitive, penetrated to the Zoo's back premises and marvelled at the appetising meals prepared for the animals, in conditions that would have put many hotel kitchens to shame.

Then on to the border country and over to the Farne Islands with a group of zoologists to see the grey seal in their rookeries. There they walked among the seal pups and saw the overcrowding and the rotting carcases of the pups who had died from starvation if their mums had mislaid them among the throng, or who had been accidentally squashed by the ungainly bulk of an adult seal rolling on them; inhaling the aroma of fish and flesh and animal excrement, and learning it was unwise to try to walk on slippery seaweed in old gumboots with worn soles. Especially when being pursued by a very large irate seal mum with teeth that wouldn't have disgraced a shark and no conception of responding to the friendly noises that humans usually find go down so well with dogs.

So the artist learned a lot. Sometimes enjoyably, like watching the pair of pine marten kept in an old aviary on the edge of Dartmoor by a retired schoolteacher, who let them out before mealtimes to play wild games in the treetops pursuing gobbets of meat attached to the end of a fishing line. Sometimes quite the reverse, like being ostracised by friends after spending an afternoon in the biology department of a

west country university with the resident stoats, whose effluvia simply would not wash off.

Sometimes enthralling, like sitting alone on a freezing afternoon in front of the plate glass window of a large water tank on a Norfolk farm, watching a pair of semi-domesticated otters disporting themselves with their supper of eels, and then with each other – perhaps to assist digestion, thought the artist naively. After about ten minutes the underwater ballet gradually became slower, the movements more languid, the caresses more sensual, tender, loving and at long last sexual. All underwater. Perhaps the most beautiful consummation it is possible to imagine.

Sometimes sad, like watching another otter, alone in a concrete prison in a large southern zoo that shall be nameless, obviously sick, trying to cool its hot nose in the greasy water of its moat, no air bubbles inside its flat, lustreless fur, and quite unable to face the rock hard slabs of frozen fish tossed over the wall by a vacant faced youth in keepers' uniform . . .

Sometimes like an unwritten scene from 'The Wind in the

Willows' – a drowsy afternoon in a punt on the river, tied up near an old boathouse, idly watching the ponies that could be seen grazing in the meadow framed by the dark tunnel of its timbers. And down among the deeply trodden hoofprints of cows and ponies by the water's edge, something like a small armoured vehicle clambered doggedly up and down the precipices and turrets of the sunbaked mud – a hedgehog who, after much trial and error, eventually found a convenient spot to drink, where its lack of any visible neck would not be too much of a handicap. With its little dark nose just above the water, it proceeded to quench its thirst with a tongue that appeared to be as pink as a cat's, and lapped just as a cat does, pausing at intervals – only during its pauses the hedgehog took the opportunity of shooting out its tongue to scoop the odd insect off leaf or grass stem . . .

And sometimes sheer magic, like the occasion on the edge of a copse in early summer, when for at least an hour the artist had been engrossed in making a background sketch, and hearing a faint rustle of leaves, looked round to find a litter of fox cubs equally engrossed in their play only fifteen yards away below the bank of the stream. Soft as thistledown they seemed as they tumbled and sprawled, their juvenile brushes fat and fluffy, paws and legs slender as if mittened in soot. Then a flash of teeth showed as the cubs tried to wrestle away a half-chewed bird's wing (pigeon or partridge?) that the most enterprising one had appropriated. This led to a vicious tug-of-war with no holds barred and much snarling – until suddenly above the bank the vixen appeared, took in the scene below and the onlooker beyond the stream in one glance and gave a muffled coughing bark that galvanised the cubs into flight. In a twinkling of an eye all the animals had vanished, leaving behind the battered bird's wing, and one breast feather that floated lazily across to land at the artist's feet.

And the paintings? I think the big company got what it wanted – mammals of Britain in their natural habitat. And not a trace of a cage or a collar, or a glass fronted tank to be seen.

Take a Pull

When beset by life's frustrations
(Traffic jams and such vexations)
Here's a recipe for getting rid of woe:
Take a pull, get memory working
There's a host of pleasures lurking
In the corners of your mind, all set to go.

Scenes and faces will come flooding . . .
Feel that youngster's heartbeats thudding
As he sees the fences looming black and tall.
Ride again that ding-dong tussle
See those eight good ponies hustle
Hear the satisfying crack of stick on ball.

Perhaps it's tea 'neath summer awnings
That attracts, or cubbing mornings
With the dawn wind nipping slyly at your ears?
Tranquil fields or breathless scurry?
Walk or gallop – Not to worry!
May the future hold new highlights down the years.

Field Lore

I wonder who first coined the aphorism 'One man's rubbish is
another man's antique?' Whoever it was certainly hit the nail
bang on the head, particularly if he (or she) had in mind the
rich harvest of outdated and unwanted farming gear – tools,
utensils, harness, transport, implements, and machinery – now
regarded as collectors' items to be honourably enshrined in
country parks and agricultural museums.

What an infinite variety of prizes there are for the
antiquarian to track down. From small and relatively simple

things like sickles, scythes, winnowing flails, butter churns, milking stools and yokes for carrying pails, to barrows, vehicles and implements of all kinds, and machines ranging from hand-operated chaff cutters or potato riddles, right up to those huge threshing machines that used to be belt-driven by panting traction engines in the rickyards. The list could go on for pages, as could the diversity of the sites from which these discarded treasures have been (or might be) gleaned. Mostly from old barns and sheds, where they may have lain for generations festooned with cobwebs and half-concealed under piles of old sacks, but sometimes dug out from the bottoms of wells, unearthed from overgrown quarries or dredged from ponds and canals, to be cleaned up and perhaps coaxed back into working order by devoted enthusiasts, amateur and professional.

Thinking back to childhood recollections of the last years of horse-powered farming, it was often hard in those days to tell what had been jettisoned as useless, and what had merely been left standing wherever it happened to be at the end of a day's work. Horse-drawn ploughs, for instance, seed drills and cultivators, and harrows, both chain and disc, were a common sight standing forlornly out in the elements apparently abandoned for good, but in fact only from the end of one tilling season to the start of the next. Not necessarily the sign of a bad farmer, merely that before the spread of tractors and low-loading trailers it wasn't easy to drag something like a plough back from an outlying field to the yard, or to the nearest shed. Machines such as grasscutters or harvesters, or anything with blades or moving parts that could be immobilised by rust even if well greased, would either be covered by a tarpaulin or stowed away under cover. But if an ageing hay-tedder or swathe turner, or a cart or a wagon, broke down, lost a wheel, or just outlived its usefulness, it was plainly a waste of effort to haul it back to the yard. Anyway, once there, where could you put it, with that long-saved-for tractor and the combine harvester and the baler, and all the gear in constant use, taking

up most of the available covered space?

So out in the fields they stayed, the once-cheerful orange, pink and blue paint flaking from cast-iron frames or lovingly carved woodwork. A plough might lie, canted tipsily, on the headland of a field beside the corduroy of ridge and furrow, taking no great harm except for the dulling of the steel share. A chain harrow, its spikes enmeshed with convolvulus, nettles and cow parsley, lurked more lethally beside hedge or drystone wall, as if waiting to entrap an unwary foxhunter taking his own line across country. A battered tumbril leaned back on its haunches with its one remaining shaft pointing skywards, like an old dog baying the moon, while another sagged with one wheel minus several spokes and a length of felloe rotted away.

Way back in the late 1940s I sat for hours sketching just such derelicts abandoned beside the rat-infested remains of a strawstack on a Hertfordshire farm, wrestling with the perspective of the massive wheels and the subtle concavity of the spokes set into the huge, ironbound hubs.

'Don't know why you want to bother with them old things,' grumbled the farmer, a formidable widow for whom beauty lay in bank notes. 'We got a lovely new float up in the yard . . .'

Lovely rubber tyres, too, Army surplus; sensible and serviceable, but not to be compared with those relics of the wainwright's and wheelwright's art. So I remained obstinately sitting on my camp stool by the strawstack, trying to ignore the rats that scampered over the dry husks ever more boldly as evening drew on.

How I wish now that I had spent far more time on sketches such as those, while the relics were still *in situ* on the farms. All credit to the artists and photographers who have made a detailed study of the subject over the years, and to the antiquarians whose efforts are ensuring that as many as possible of the artefacts from the era of the working horse and the early years of mechanised farming will be preserved for the foreseeable future. Tribute must also be paid to the voluntary bodies who organise ploughing matches and thus keep alive the ploughman's art, and encourage the skills of working two, three and four horses in chain gear, to harrows, rollers or cultivators.

The breed societies, and the brewers, have certainly done a magnificent job in keeping the heavy horse breeds both pure and in the public eye. But those superbly glossy, corned-up teams that are driven so expertly round show rings, or which delight the crowds by their musical drive with harrows at the Horse of the Year Show, are as glamorous as film stars in comparison to the vast majority of unsung work horses who spent their lives on the average farm. Sweat-streaked coats, mud-stained 'feather', long, tangled manes and forelocks and inadequate tails. Not an ounce of spare flesh – almost gaunt at the end of the harvest season, after long hours in the fields

without much water. To the eyes of a child, they were huge gentle, dusty creatures in shabby harness, plodding endlessly up and down vast brown fields, ears permanently half back to catch the words of command from ploughman or waggoner, or perhaps standing with an old miller's sack thrown over their loins as they chewed meditatively at their midday bait. A winter recollection: four horses hauling a timber wagon along a muddy woodland ride, the air round them steaming from their heavy breathing and the sweat from their backs. A more peaceful scene with a wise old mare between the shafts of a cart, no one at her head as she moved slowly from one pile of swedes to the next, while the team of labourers deftly topped and tailed the roots and cast them with unerring aim into the cart. Or a breathless summer evening with Spitfires wheeling over the harvest fields, and thunderheads building up. A wagon with a pair of tired Shires, the trace-horse ostensibly under the command of a diminutive child, the shaft-horse half hidden by the sheaves of corn drooping from the forehead of the wagon as it slowly processed from stook to stook in a bid to clear the field before the weather broke. . .

Were the horses really so massive as memory portrays

them? Old photographs show that many working horses must
have been well under sixteen hands, and light enough to have
done a milk round as well as working in the fields. Of course, in
the Highlands and the Pennines, on the hill farms of Wales,
and in Ireland, strong ponies of around fourteen hands and
with plenty of bone – Highland, Dales, Fell, Welsh Cob and
Connemara – were widely used. And no matter where he lived,
a farmer on poor land, struggling to make ends meet, had to
make do with whatever draught animals were available,
sometimes teaming a pony or a smallish horse with a donkey or
a mule, or even a heifer, on whose short neck a horsecollar sat
incongruously. A far cry from the yoked teams of oxen used in
earlier times, the last survivors of which were still to be seen in
Cirencester Park until the early 1960s.

Much depended on the type and quality of the travelling
stallions which, led by their handlers, plodded through the
country lanes from one farm to the next, as well as on what
bargains in horseflesh the farmer could pick up at the horse
fairs, or on what the gipsies might bring down the lane tied to
the tail of their van. The larger farmers, with their own stallion,
could breed for type and quality, and their carters, each doing

two horses, were under discipline almost as strict in its own way as lads in a racing stable – and were just as proud of 'their' horses.

But perfect matching for colour, type and size was only the icing on the cake. Greys, bays, roans, blacks and even the occasional pie, clean legged or with varying amounts of feather, could and did work in perfect harmony with each other and with their man – stride and temperament being more important than mere size. The bond between a good horseman and his team could amount almost to telepathy, and gave to the man a fulfilment that made up for much of the hardship of his life. And the rivalry of one farm with another at the annual ploughing matches was the spur that motivated all those extra hours of grooming, of plaiting manes and tails with braids of green and yellow or red, white and blue wool, the oiling of hooves, and the polishing and burnishing of best harness and brasses – if best sets existed.

And now the remnants of some of those sets of harness, from the plainest and shabbiest, with the stuffing poking out through the holes worn in the faded duster check lining of collar or pad, to the most ornate, with tooled leather and intricate brass or steel ornamentation, are preserved, neatly labelled, on the whitewashed walls of museums. So are the

rows of wagons and carts, the machinery and the implements –
not only documenting where they were acquired, but who
made them and when, and sometimes annotating in detail
individual features and quirks of style that identify the maker
like the brushwork on an old master's canvas.

The ranks of today's experts have been swelled, too, by the
model-makers, who preserve something of the old skills in
miniature. So woe betide the artist who cheats and puts a
Norfolk wagon into a Cotswold scene, or a Welsh sled into a
Devonshire valley, or peaked northern collars on a team in a
southern setting!

But was the down-to-earth reality of farming ever quite so
precise as some of the experts would have us believe? Excep-
tions prove the rule, they say. . .

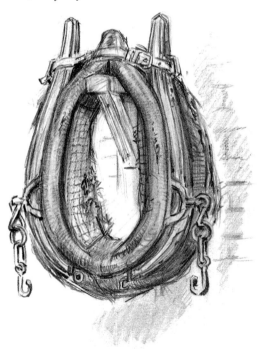

Girl in Blue Jeans

Through the dawn comes, softly riding,
    The brownest of colleens,
She sits an Arab pony and
    Wears faded old blue jeans.
She waves to me, then calls her dogs
    And disappears from view . . .
Was it a dream? If so, who made
    Those tracks etched in the dew?

Shepherds

Winter evening on the fell,
Bright stars gleaming – who can tell
What they saw two thousand years ago?

Other shepherds, other sheep
Roused by brightness out of sleep,
Wondering 'Should we follow, should we go?'

Rocking

Here I am a-rocking
On my gallant wooden gee
But inside me I'm a-hawking
With companions two or three.

Here I come a-pricking
With sword and lance to hand –
Or perhaps I'll try pig-sticking
In India's dusty land.

Here I am a-wandering
Alone without a care –
Next moment I'm philandering
'Cause girls all look so fair.

Here we are surrounded,
Mid battle's smoke and roar –
And both of us are wounded,
Along with plenty more . . .

Here we are back home again
And just in time for tea –
Never more to roam again,
My dear old steed and me . . .

    . . . at least, not until tomorrow!

Tony-Pony

'Well, they call me a Family Pony
    Safe both to ride and to drive –
But that's really a load of baloney,
    No PONY would ever survive!

'I'm a pram with a built-in computer
    That knows when enough is enough.
I'm a nannie-cum-watchdog-cum-tutor
    And just once in a way I get tough.

'It's a good thing for them there's no union
    To tell me to strike or protest –
But just sometimes I do wish they'd tune in
    And listen to what *I* like the best:

'Now I *do* like my apples in quarters
    'Cause my teeth aren't quite what they were,
And I'm *not* keen on strangers' small daughters
    Who tickle my tum with a straw.

'If I trample your sack, or egg or balloon
    At gymkhanas, *don't* get in a tiz,
Just find me some shade on a hot afternoon
    And leave me in peace for a ziz.

'And at shows, if I flatten the fences
    Or shy, or run out or refuse –
I've not taken leave of my senses,
    I'm just teaching the young how to lose!'

Suckers. . .

The old mare foaled in the longest night
   And died in the chill of dawn's first light.
But the foal was alive and struggled to stand
   To suck warm milk from a kindly hand.

He was small and his hide was crumpled and creased
   But the energy flowed like an imp released
Till his legs gave way and he folded up
   And went to sleep like a weary pup.

The boy, so they said, was not too bright.
   His schoolmates jeered but he wouldn't fight.
'Wally!' they said, and 'Dummy!' and 'Pratt!'
   With the age-old malice of brat to brat.

Then one of them, versed in gangster talk
   Wrote 'Wally's a sucker!' in blackboard chalk.
But the boy just smiled: 'Thee wait and see
   If we're not *prize* suckers, t'colt and me!'

Ears

Ears to prick
And ears to flick
To listen and look and learn.

Ears that are quick
To warn of a kick,
Or a stranger's touch to spurn.

Ears that greet
Or ask for a treat,
And welcome a friend's return.

The Opportunist

Little fat dog, one ear white, one ear brown,
Lolling pink tongue – he's a bit of a clown.
How did he get there, and can he jump down?

Whether . . .

Whether you jump
Or 'event' or bump
Or loyally stand and wait,
May the luck of the day
Always come your way –
May you fly every five-barred gate.

The music of hounds
Or a dozen clear rounds,
Oblivion or sweet success;
A promising hack
Or a nice rein back
Or a muzzle's soft caress . . .

If horses give
You the spice to live
In work, or sport, or leisure –
May each year's run
Be a joyous one,
With memories to treasure.

Quartette

The dashing chaser, head on high
    Told of his triumphs – 'There was I,
Baulked at the Brook, but in the straight
    I showed 'em how to carry weight!'

The war horse rolled a fiery eye
    Dreaming of battles – 'There was I,
The equine tank . . . ah, Chivalry,
    The very name revolves round me.'

The pony, tossing tangled hair,
    Neighed 'Ere they bred you, I was there!
When man chased mammoths 'neath the sky,
    And painted caverns – there was I.'

The donkey pricked his patient ears
    As memories drifted down the years . . .
Then spoke: 'I heard a child's first cry,
    And by His manger, there was I.'